Songs Of Silence

Suman Shekhawat

Made with ❤ on the BookLeaf Publishing Platform
www.bookleafpub.in
www.bookleafpub.com

Dedication

THIS BOOK IS DEDICATED TO MY FATHER,
COL B.S. RATHORE, WHO OFTEN BELIVES IN ME
MORE THAN I DO IN MYSELF.

Preface

My love for poetry began during my master's in English literature, transforming from a subject of study into a passion that now shapes how I see the world.

As a keen observer of nature, people and animals, I find inspiration in the simplest yet most profound moments- a moving breeze, a wildflower, a glance with a stranger, or silent loyalty in an animal's eyes.

My poetry is deeply rooted in real-life experiences, relationships and emotions .
This book is not just a collection of my thoughts but a mirror in which I hope readers see a part of themselves.

May these poems speak to you as much as they have spoken to me.

Suman Shekhawat

Acknowledgements

With the deepest gratitude, I wish to thank every soul who has walked into my life. This book is reflection of countless stories, conversations and experiences I've shared with people. Each encounter whether joyful or painful, have left an imprint on my heart, and helped in shaping my poem.

I would like to thank my husband, *Narendra* for being my pillar of strength and for his support in whatever I do.
I would like to thank my big brother, *Devendra Singh* for patiently listening to my poems before publishing, thank you for always having faith in me.
My precious sisters, *Sushil,* whose love and support knows no limit.. *Saroj, and Shivani* thank you for always being there.

My special thanks to my parents and in-laws for their endless blessings. Gratitude to my late grandfather. whose knowledge and love continue to shine in my life.

My heartfelt thanks to *Bookleaf publishers*, for giving such an amazing platform. Their guidance and insight shaped this journey.

And finally my kids. *Ishan and Jiya,* who pushed me to complete this book. they are my critic and motivator, which helped in creation of this book.

With profound gratitude
Suman,

1. Morning Tea

Deep in thought,
kiss of the morning breeze,
listening to the susurration of nature,
And cuppa tea in my hand
Here, I'm rejoicing my morning potion,
every sip taking away my drowsiness,
rejuvenating every part of me.

Whether I'm at hills or desert
Whether its spring or autumn,
happy or gloomy,
the first cuppa tea is must for me,
nothing gonna replace it,
its either TEA or nothing.

here, I;m relishing it,
all alone by myself
engrossed in thoughts of one,
who is far,far away,
still so close

As distance doesn't matter between you and me.

thanks to TEA, as you refresh my mind,
and my memories too,
reminds me of my love...

i know soon I'll be with him....
sipping together,
our morning TEA.

2. My Angel sleeps

sh ! ssh! My angel sleeps,
so calm, so serene,
she keeps,
one more day of fun and frolicking,
one more day of giggling and whining,
passed by....

she looks so radiant,
in bright moonlight,
I plea, O' wind, don't be in rush
let the murmur of night,
be lullaby for my angel.

there she sleeps tight,
to see this ethereal sight,
I am awake whole night.

3. Hills Of Haldighati

As I was travelling,
I crossed through hills,
they are no ordinary hills,
"hills of Haidighati"
I was passing by,,,,

Plethora of emotions,
hope, fear, pride
joy and sadness, side by side.

I'm a dreamer,
boundless are my imagination,
As I pass by,
I could hear, whispers of hills
there are stories to be told,
but few are listeners on this road....

With the breeze,
among the rustling leaves,
I could hear hoofbeats....

On the lone hill, there stands a radiant blue horse,
under the blue sky.
Not just any horse,
bards of his trust and valour are sung,
in the realms of his Master.

In my boundless imagination,
we had wordless communication.....

i heard tale of sacrifice,
tale of pledge unspoken,
tale of bond unbroken,
taking a dip in the ocean of emotion....

i bow down to you noble free spirit...
i bow down to hills of Haldighati....

4. My Terrace Garden

I have a terrace garden,
full of greens,
which I have gathered over time.
some are old,
some are dying,
making space for young ones to shine.

It is a retreat for me
where I sit and sip,
take nature's dip.

Finding my solace in listening to songs of nature,
chirping of birds,
buzzing bees,
chattering squirrels,
rustling leaves, with whispering breeze.
such a flawless blend,
I call all of them, my morning friend.

5. Song of Silence

Have you ever listened to silence ?
leaving behind the cacophony of mundane life.

Have you ever wondered that part of you is lost ?
in the hustle - bustle of cities

Have you ever yearn for solitude?
may be a quite moment with yourself.
quieter you become more you hear.
may be you overcome all your fear,
and everything becomes clear.

Have you ever sat alone, without being lonely?
and felt all unexpressed emotion.
so, listen to song of silence,
and enjoy the moment of catharsis.
embrace your own company.

once you start enjoying 'song of silence'
you will learn to 'dance without music'.

6. Bubbles o bubbles

Bubbles o bubbles!
soaring high up to the sky
will you be my message bearer for a day
I know it's not easy,
hurdles to pass by...
you are like a beautiful orb,
moving around like free spirit.
people might want to touch you,
then and there your life is done,
so change your path for me.

Oh dear!
on your way, don't get dazzled by the beauty of flowers,
sometimes they come with thorns,
just a peck and you finished forever.
Your nature is to wander, not rest,
so soar high up to the sky,
you are no less,
you hold the rainbow within yourself.

Those tiny- tots will run after you,
your beauty mesmerizes them too,
so change your path for me.
as you carry my message.
A message to almighty,
who created you and me.
A message of gratitude, that,
"life is beautiful and blessed I feel,
thank you for giving me all".

7. Blank Canvass

Few blank canvass lying in my room,
wonder, are they staring at me,
or I'm staring at them.
Let me pick up one from the pile,
set it up on my frame,
Now is the time,
Momentarily smile flickered over, it was short-lived
and fear took over.
I looked at blank canvass,
bittersweet feeling hovering over.

Blank canvass like barren land,
with endless possibilities' in my hand

Blank canvas like a new stage,
where I have to perform,
but butterflies fluttering inside me....
My mighty brushes ready to embrace hues
together they are ready to sway,
happily my way.....

8. Girl With Heart Of Gold

There is this girl in my lane,
everyone knows her,
she's got some different fame,
stays just three blocks away,
with dogs she play.

Something common we share,
for dogs we love and care
though we never spoke,
but a friendly smile was always there.

she feeds stray dogs at home
because on roads other social animals roam.
She gives them a warm bed when it's cold,
she's got a heart of gold.

Something common we share,
for dogs we love and care.
She fought battles to keep them safe.
she is so bold.

i wish I could do the same.
but I'm scared of getting trolled,
as people here are too shallow,
they think these lanes are for humans
and dog should not follow.

I bet you ask dog,
they will say ; " there is this ANGEL who lives here
among HUMANS,
for her, they wag their tail and follow.

9. In Memory

Long ago you've gone
sometimes I still mourn,
your memories are still safe in a section of my thoughts,
memories that try to fade away,
but my heart won't let them sway.

Endless stories that you've told,
stories of birds and bees, kings and queens,
still, come to my dreams.
Nickname which you gave me, I still hold.
But how will I quench my thirst to hear them once
more?

The village used to be so much fun,
when you were around,
now there is a huge void, which I fill with my silent cry,
and a tear drop fell from the side of my eye.

I know we will meet once more,
when my life here is done,

you will be there to welcome me at heaven's door
again we will sit and chat a lot more...

P.S.: In memory of my grandfather.

10. Morning Walk

Morning walks are special,
you meet all sorts of people,

young and old, sick and suave,
men and women, some couples

Fast walkers zoom like they're in race
while slow ones move at turtle's pace

some are not interested in walk,
but they do talk and like to stalk.

while few sit cross-legged, chanting mantra's
experts performing yoga sutra's

one who walks backwards, claims it best
but what if he bumps into pole ?

few are lost in thoughts of work and home,
their mind just roams, even at rest.

Tree lovers gazing up to branches,
with every plant their vibe matches,

some walk dogs, they two happily chat
while dog haters frown - imagine that.

that one man strides ahead of all, with pride
as if he owns the path so wide

our veterans boast days gone by
with endless tales, remembering fallen comrades they
cry.

and then myself. thinking about
A world within a single park
while my morning walk

11. Moon Dance

Now I am fine
but when I die,
don't put my ashes in the holy river,
but scatter them in our garden,
then sow some seeds
watch the tree growing out of my ashes
let birds sit and sing melodies for you.
cherish memories and sip tea
under the shade of the tree
and chat with me in silence.
In the night,
adorn the tree with fairy light,
hold your glass tight,
pour our favourite wine.
with our friends, dance to our tune,
that has to be 'MOON DANCE'
you will feel me dancing with the swing of branches and
leaves.
I will be always with you as a tree,

12. Grandfather's cupboard

In the corner, quite and still,
bulky, blue cupboard stands,
everything around is changed,
but Grandfather's cupboard stands
with stories to spill.
once the heart of his room
now left alone, bearing silent pain,
its colour has faded
but brightening my memories,
cupboard full of herbal cure, with a bittersweet smell
all handy tools he used to keep,
cupboard full of solutions
reminds me of those toffees and sweets tucked in a
hidden place
that used to be our prize for good deeds,
giving everyone an equal piece, with your hand you used
to feed,
nothing in the world tasted so sweet.
Those wrinkled hands and the jingling keys,
guarding his treasure with ease

oh! That frowning gaze when keys went astray,
now those keys lost their charm,
key and cupboard rarely meet.
now no more secret treat.
holding memories of yesteryear,
Grandfather's cupboard still stands there.

13. Wildflower

Have you ever sensed the beauty of wildflowers?
I wonder who put those seeds
they bloom with minimal needs,
in a secluded urn or a barren land
without a helping hand,
storms may bend them,
Sun may burn,
plucked by strangers
or crushed under feet,
yet with each dawn, they return in fleet,
dancing with the breeze,
living in ease
maybe they teach us to flourish, whatever life may throw
like a wildflower find your light in the darkest of places
let no storm break your strength apart
and grow wherever you go.

14. Spring Is Here

The warmth of the sun is spreading,
winter chills are fading,
new hope and new blooms,
after long winter glooms.

Butterflies visit every row of bud,
telling them to unfold,
as spring is here.

Old tattered leaves fallen.
soft warm rays of the Sun
welcoming the arrival of new ones.

Birds chirping at the top of their voice,
singing songs in rejoice,
as spring is here.

Red carnations spreading the love around,
sunflowers smiling at the glimpse of sun.

Every other flower is ready to blossom.
The happiness which spring brings has no bound.

15. Before Dawn

The sun is yet to rise and shine
I choose this time, only to be mine
When Morning Star is about to say goodbye,
waiting fir Sun to say hi!
Just before the dawn,
when everyone else is sleeping,
cosmos is listening,
time to speak about wishes and wounds,
may the universe will conspire to fulfill
maybe it becomes moment of epiphany,
time to get clarity from a cluttered mind.
Every new morning is like a blank page,
fill it with colourful happy memories.

16. Ancient marvel-Aravalli's

The mighty mountains of Aravalli ranges
oldest of all, protecting us from ages.
An ancient marvel, witnessing the change of civilization.
which is beyond human imagination.

In folds of mountains, centuries of stories to unfold
home for birds and beast
treasure for mankind
but polluted is man's mind
he is not satisfied kind

They dig and dig. till they reach the core
took out every ore.
for cities and skyscrapers
every inch of the mountain they scrape

Rivers are lost and dead
which Aravalli once held.
extracting everything from its lap

when did our hearts become so black?

don't we fear nature's backlash
its just a matter of snap,
we can become a heap of trash.
nature's wrath, storm, thunder,
barren land, no drop of water,
are we ready to take all?

my heart weeps, when
mortals try crushing immortals.

17. Who am I?

I am One,
yet different for everyone,
no one knows my true self,
for some, I'm quiet and shy,
others think I talk way too high,
at times I'm so intense,
pain of dying leaf I can sense,
but I'm also one who doesn't care for details.
They say I'm wise and mature,
close ones know I'm a kid at heart for sure.
Am I a thinker,
but about a few things I don't want to think at all..
Few know me as an artist,
for some, I'm a poet.
I'm a dancing queen, In my dreams.
there are days I look for parties.
but then yearns for solitude, seeing life in cities.
Maybe that's how women are in their forties,
but I left part of me in my twenties.
For society, I may be a mother, daughter

wife, sister or just a woman.
can't do much about ever judging men,
Beneath all these layers, somewhere lies my true self,
maybe a bit of all, but not stagnant
I'm ever-evolving,
and that is only for me to explore.

18. It Must Be Women Driving

On the city road, on the highway
how easy for you to say,
that must be a woman driving,
too slow, too fast or just perfect,
always judging her pace,
passing that smile so sly.
But it was a chaotic day for her,
her mind's in a race
a thousand worries she cannot erase.
List of chores in her heart, deep sunk
decluttering of that messy trunk,
groceries low, pantry decayed
hope kids love the supper she made
what about friends meet,
delaying since last week.
Her hands on steering,
managing both car and home with zeal
So next time give her a little way,
before you curse, before you sigh

think of the weight she carries inside,
women driving is more than it seems,
she is holding steering of her family, her hopes and
dreams.

19. Life

Life is an experience
filled with adventures, to overcome fears,
with every bold step, we reach new heights,
whether its day or starry night,

Life is an experience
full of ups and downs
Joy and misery may come and go
to cleanse our souls.

Life is experience,
embrace as it comes.

20. Bliss - my dog

You came into my life,
we named you "Bliss"
and indeed, you proved it right,
became the bliss of our life.
With a wagging tail and sparkling eyes,
you loved us beyond the skies,
playing tug of war
keeping the kid in us alive,

A warm welcome at the door,
lifting our spirits even more.
our walks together is a must,
where new friends we meet
love how you enjoy your treat.
Now no need for words
I can read your eyes , and you mine.
You must be part of my past,
a bond so strong,
forever it will last.

21. Journey

We are but travellers,
for same destination,
we take different paths,
on journey called life,
with no map to guide.

On this journey, we meet, fellow travellers,
call them friends, family or maybe enemies,
some in search of soulmates,
while others walk alone.

Love, kindness, faith
anger jealousy, hatred,
pick up with what, you want to fill the baggage
b,coz all which we claim,
house, land, riches
will be left behind

for the final path none can defy,
rich or poor, fame or no name,

we all must say goodbye.
in the end, when all is done,
The journey ends where it once begun.

22. My Poem

If you want to know me,
go through my poems.
I pour my heart,
in my verses,
read all lines,
but don't miss to read between the lines,
there are hidden signs....
If you are a friend or acquaintance
find yourself in my poems,
things I adore,
things I abhor,
I wrote about all,
tried to open my heart's door.